Miriam Colón

Actor and Theater Founder

Written by Mayra Fernández

Illustrated by Luis Arvelo

MODERN CURRICULUM PRESS

Program Reviewers

Anna M. López, Director,
    Bilingual Education and Foreign
    Languages
    Perth Amboy Public Schools
    Perth, Amboy, New Jersey

Kerima Swarz, Instructional Support
    Teacher
    Philadelphia School District
    Philadelphia, Pennsylvania

Eva Teagarden, Bilingual Resource
    Specialist
    Yuba City Unified School District
    Yuba City California

Gladys White, Bilingual Program
    Manager
    East Baton Rouge Parish School
    Board
    Baton Rouge, Louisiana

MODERN CURRICULUM PRESS

13900 Prospect Road, Cleveland, Ohio 44136

A Paramount Publishing Company

ISBN 0-8136-5265-0 (Reinforced Binding)   0-8136-5271-5 (Paperback)

Library of Congress Catalog Card Number: 93-79434

Dear Readers,

Miriam Colón loves two things: the theater and her people. To her the theater is magic: to make believe and have people come to watch her, to have them laugh or cry. She studied her art well.

After much hard work, this Puerto Rican also helps others by bringing her theater—the magic—to the people in their own neighborhoods. Isn't that fun!

Your friend,

Mayra Fernández

Miriam Colón watched the actors on the stage, her eyes open wide. It was 1950 and she was only five years old, but already Miriam knew she wanted to be an actor. She wanted to be part of the exciting world of the theater.

Miriam lived with her parents in Ponce, Puerto Rico. Miriam had always looked forward to going to school to learn to read and write. After she saw her first play, she knew she wanted to learn to be an actor, too.

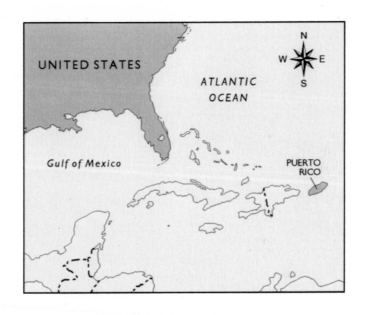

When she was about six years old Miriam began taking acting lessons. She studied and practiced her acting very hard. Miriam thought nothing could be more wonderful than acting in front of an audience. She wanted to make people smile and enjoy themselves.

Miriam was a good actress right from the start. When she was only eight years old, she was given a part in a play in New York City. It was her first big acting job.

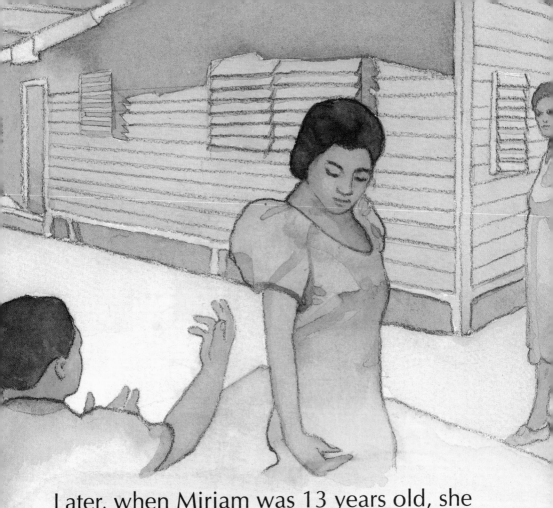

Later, when Miriam was 13 years old, she
began taking theater classes at the University
of Puerto Rico. There Miriam joined a theater
group that traveled from place to place. The
group put on plays in cities and towns all over
Puerto Rico.

7 AV
IMPERIAL
IMPERIAL
Piscator
Dramatic
Workshop
Technical Institute

While she studied, Miriam was asked to be in some other stage plays and television shows in the United States. When she was about eighteen, Miriam studied at a well-known acting school in New York. Going to this school was a very big honor for her.

In New York, Miriam was also asked to join the famous Actors Studio. She was the first Puerto Rican to become a part of that acting group.

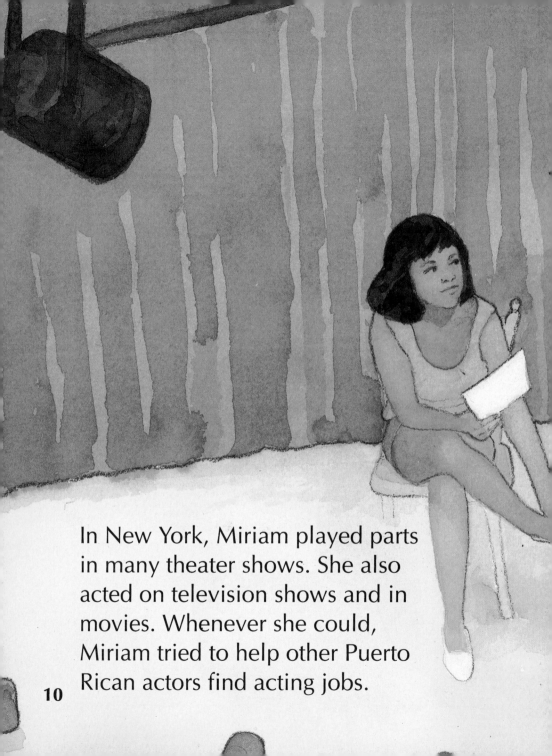

In New York, Miriam played parts in many theater shows. She also acted on television shows and in movies. Whenever she could, Miriam tried to help other Puerto Rican actors find acting jobs.

11

Miriam found that in New York there were not very many acting jobs for Hispanic Americans. In the early 1960s, Miriam and a friend formed an acting group for Hispanic actors. This group was one of the first to give Hispanic actors a place to perform in New York.

Miriam wanted to do more to bring Hispanic theater to all Americans. In 1967, she and her husband, George Edgar, founded an acting group that put on plays in the poorer neighborhoods of New York. It was called the Puerto Rican Traveling Theater, or PRTT.

Most of the plays that the Traveling Theater performed were written by Hispanic people about their lives. At first the plays were presented in English. Later they were also presented in Spanish.

The theater group performed its plays in the streets for all to see. Its first play was *The Oxcart*, presented in 1967. It was written by a well-known Puerto Rican named René Marqués.

19

In 1974, Miriam decided she would find one place for her traveling group to perform. She looked and looked for a perfect place. Finally, she found just the right spot—a building that was once a fire station! The Puerto Rican Traveling Theater gives plays in that same building today.

For over thirty years, Miriam Colon has given her time to the growing Hispanic theater in the United States. When she is not acting in plays, Miriam helps to direct plays.

Miriam has also spent many hours teaching acting to children. She wants others to feel the thrill she felt when she started acting.

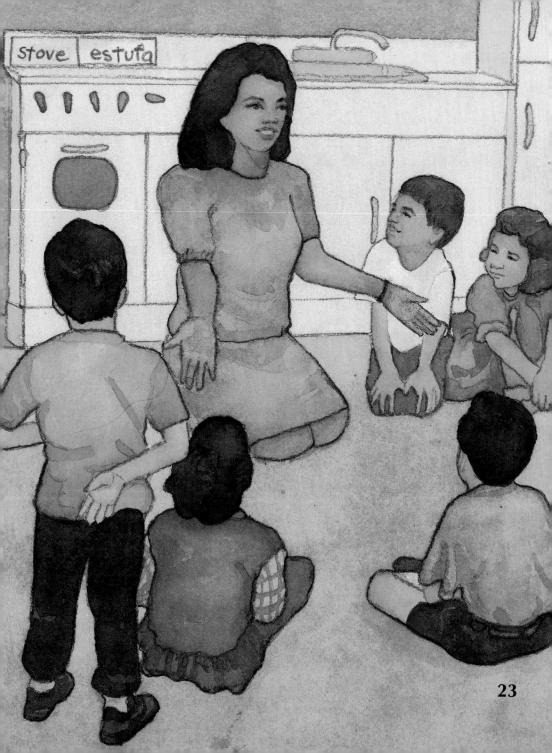

23

Miriam Colón has received many awards for her work in the theater. In 1990, she was given the White House Hispanic Heritage Award.

Today, Miriam is still a part of the wonderful world of the theater. If you are in New York, stop by the old fire station and watch one of her plays!

Glossary

actor (ak' tər) A person who plays a part or acts in a play, movie, or television show

founder (foun' dər) A person who establishes something

perform (pər fôrm) To present or act out

Puerto Rico (pwer' tō rē' kō) An island in the Caribbean. It is a part of the United States, officially called the Commonwealth of Puerto Rico. It has its own governor and its own flag. The people born there are U.S. citizens.

studio (stoo' dē ō) A room or building where an actor or artist works

theater (thē' ə tər) A place where plays or movies are shown

About the Author

Mayra Fernández is a teacher in East Los Angeles, California. Dr. Fernández has been teaching for 27 years. She has twelve children, six of whom are adopted. Three of the adopted children are Mexican-American, one is Cuban, one Nicaraguan, and one Pakistani. All form a rainbow of love around her life. Dr. Fernández is kept busy teaching, writing poetry and stories, and giving workshops to parents and teachers. She dedicates this book to her daughter Suni, one of her rainbow children.

About the Illustrator

A graduate of Pratt Institute, Luis Arvelo is presently doing graduate work in art education while teaching in the Yonkers Public Schools and doing freelance illustrations for corporations, medical magazines, and book publishers. He has also created a series of collector Christmas stamps. For *Miriam Colón*, his first children's book, he worked in watercolor.